Just B|

Poems, Prose, Quotes and Art

ISBN: 978-1-913479-49-7 (paperback)
ISBN: 978-1-913479-50-3 (ebook)

That Guy's House
20-22 Wenlock Road
London
England
N1 7GU

www.thatGuysHouse.com

Beth was a talented, beautiful young woman with a great future ahead of her. She was a designer for Google, having just finished her apprenticeship and winning Apprentice of the Year. Creativity flowed through her, and she spent a lot of her free time playing the piano and guitar, writing poetry, singing at open mic nights, painting and designing.

It hadn't always been that way because as a teenager, Beth struggled with finding her own identity as a young woman; she wanted to succeed and do/be her best at all times. This constant pressure she put herself under took her through a period of time where she suffered with anxiety, and during her darkest moments, she took to self-harm as the feeling of 'not being good enough' took over. At this time, she started to write poetry as a form of therapy. Beth's creativity enabled her to put pen to paper, capturing the real, raw emotion of the most difficult situations, drawing the reader in and enabling them to feel and understand how difficult life can be as a young adult growing up in the world as it is today. Although quite dark, her writing and art truly depict the experiences of herself and others who shared their deepest, darkest moments with her. Very suddenly, in 2018 Beth lost her Nan who was only 65; it was at that time Beth wrote 'An Ode to Young Death' and 'The Fear of Becoming Old'.

As well as her passion for the arts, Beth cared deeply about people and animals. She truly believed that there was good in everyone and that people should just be themselves; this was clearly demonstrated in the diverse range of friendship groups that she had in her life. She would always go out of her way to help those less fortunate than herself, or who were just struggling every day, despite her own life being chaotic; because as she said, 'that's how creative people rolled' and she wanted to give something back where she could. Beth had an infectious personality; she was good-natured, crazy, loved to dance, and she lit up a room with her presence, touching the souls of everyone she met. She was at one with nature, and in particular, had a real fondness for bees, and their existence in this world was important to her.

Just as it felt like Beth had all things going her way – with an amazing job, deposit for a house, and having the time of her life – she was unfortunately involved in a tragic accident where she was taken from us in May 2019, age 21.

In her memory, I wanted to share with you her work. Beth would never have been brave enough to get any of this printed herself. The work within this book, will, I am sure, resonate with someone at some point in their lives, and if only one piece brings you some comfort, help, or makes you smile, then I have continued to carry on Beth's legacy.

With Love, Beth's Mum x

LINKS & OTHER THINGS
CLOSE TO BETH'S HEART

ylf.org.uk
The Young Lives Foundation

bumblebeeconservation.org
Bumblebee Conservation

porchlight.org.uk
Kent's largest charity for homeless
and vulnerable people

chrisriversart.com
Artwork by Chris Rivers

Books

Lanny – Max Porter

The Little Pocket Book of Crystal Chakra Healing
– *Philip Permutt*

Eleanor Oliphant is completely Fine
– *Gail Honeyman*

ZAMI – A bio mythography
- *Audre Lorde*

The Book you Wish your Parents had Read (and your children will be glad that you did)
– *Philippa Perry*

Inspirational Music Artists

Florence +The Machine, The Killers, Amy Winehouse, Daughter, Cyn, Billie Eillish, Bon Iver, The Fugees, London Grammar & last but not least – She loved Netflix

CONFUSION

My personality is a jumble of things,
A confusion of what I'm fighting not to be,
And a metaphorical delusion of what I want to be
tomorrow.
An 18 year process of shedding skins like a snake,
Being no way nearer to the resolution I wanted.
Or what the fuck I'm meant to be doing with my life.
Decisions after decisions pressed down on me like a
Weight.
When I only have one true answer, and that is,
'I have no fucking clue.'

ODE TO YOUNG DEATH

When you think about death,
You know it is inevitable,
But you never realise,
That you are just breathing to die.

When people talk about dying,
You believe that it will happen
One day coming,
But it's never going to be tomorrow.

When a loved one is dying,
You will not believe the truth,
Or the tragedy of it all,
Until you find their to-do-list left full.

When a loved one is dead,
You will ask why you are not,
Realising life is wasted,
On work, hurt, and too many cigarettes.

I try to fragment together, the amount of time we laughed,
Or screamed our goodbyes.
I try to remember myself,
How I was when I was intertwined,
With you.
But nothing comes close,
To the shaking breath of our bodies,
Crashing into each other,
Nothing ever comes close,
To that full feeling that I felt
When we drank coffee together.
I cannot remember the exact time,
That I stopped loving you.
I can't remember the seconds
Spent thinking us through,
But I can remember falling,
For your eyes and lasting smile,
I remember us well.

The sun sets, over thin clouds,
That disperse into thin air,
Another day done,
Do you even care?
The sun is sleeping, overtaken,
By darkness that shrouds,
The sun away, done,
Empty carcasses of clouds,
Air sucked from the lungs,
Of a poor soulless ghost,
That is searching the darkness,
For a way out,
Done.
I don't even care

ADDICTION

I'm addicted to you
But you make me feel alone
I'm addicted to you
But you are addicted to coke

Take me back
To before we met
Let me go
So that I can forget

Where's my head
I think you stole it
Give it back
Before I've lost it

I'm addicted to you
But your feelings never show
I'm addicted to you
But you like being alone

At the edge
It's the way you look,
Into my eyes
When you lay me down

I'll have nothing
If I can't have you,

I'm intent,
On holding us down

Take me back,
To before we met,
Let me go,
So I can forget

I'm addicted to you
You made me cheat death,
I'm addicted to you
But can't catch my breath

I want to
Believe that it's true
But no change
To seasons, change you

Take me back
To before we met
Let me go
So that I can forget

And just like that he appeared...
But I told you I wasn't ready
And the symbol of love,
Was replaced,
By a rose tarnished machete

I WONDER

I wonder what it would be like
To be a woman who has been with a man
That has always put her first
and brought her up, when she was down.

I wonder what it would be like
To walk into a room full of people
and feel the one pair of eyes
you treasure the most, see you, first.

I see women filled to the brim
with confidence, as they walk and talk
and smile as if they hold
The whole damn world in their hearts.

I wonder what it would be like
To not have been cursed by words,
Laid down upon my heart,
by the same man, that lays me down.

I see women knowing only good men,
Doing wonderful things with their hearts,
Giving themselves to other
good men after,
and other good men after,
Without any trouble.

I see women knowing their worth,
Not settling for another bad fit,
Not settling for another bad guy, after bad guy,
After bad decisions.

I see myself settling for what I know,
Settling for another bad guy,
Another bad fit,
Thinking that a bad fit,
Is the only thing I deserve.

FIXATION

I watch you,
My eyes fall down
To how you move
I'm fixated

I feel you,
Step towards me
I step forward
Into your space

How do you like
To be taken down,
You can have me,
Just be straightforward
Don't knock my crown

I can give you
What you desire
Lay you down
The right way,

I see the hunger,
Animalistic ways
When you watch me,
Captivated

I see you, talk
with your tongue
Let's serve each other
With liquid phrases

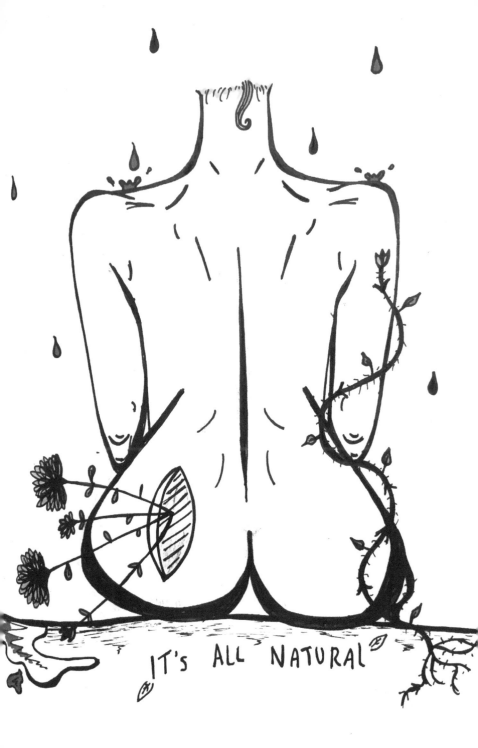

IT's ALL NATURAL

Throughout my life I see men, as
The revolving door of a woman's life
Women degrading themselves to be less
of a being, to turn a man on

I constantly battle with myself,
On whether I am independent,
Or independent on the idea, of,
Feeling independent

The idea of letting myself love a
Man is simply the worst way
Of degrading myself
and becoming, average

The idea of depending on someone
Is simply the worse way of making myself
Feel true, happiness

The idea of losing my own self control
For it to be twisted and tormented,
Is forever torturous

I will be forever in awe of people,
who are happy together
In a simplistic and natural way

I will be forever longing for someone
To help me, love myself.

In the way that I love others

I will never let myself hurt someone
In the way that I have been,
So, carelessly, hurt

I will never let myself be vulnerable
To another man who, will,
Ultimately be my downfall

I will always be on the side-lines,
Of my own brain,
Telling myself that loving is easy

I will always be left alone by pushing
Pushing people too far,
Pushing people away,
Pushing myself to the brink

My thoughts,
Suspended on a pedestal
Of regret,
And hatred,
Towards myself
Suspended!

REGRET

If it hadn't been too soon,
I could have learnt you,
taught myself to let go,
And revel in your being.
If I hadn't blamed it on you,
I could have spoken,
my anguished, hurt words,
And lay with you in bed,
Sinking, softly into a slumber,
I could have learnt, to
love the way you made
my breath shake with desire.
I couldn't admit to you how,
you owned me.
When I felt ashamed by
never feeling like this before.
You had all of me,
And I forced you to give up,
And love someone else,
As if I hated your every essence.
And I cowered away from you
And the way my stomach concaved,
And my lungs ached,
And my heart dissolved, into oblivion,

Of self-hatred
Of desire for you
For you to be mine again
I still feel like death
and no other sex will make
me let us go,
You have me strung on a pedestal.

HURT

Hurting comes naturally to me
Hurt is a phrase that encompasses my brain
It plays on my mind, tortures my soul,
But refuses to spit me out again.

I have never remembered a year,
Where I have not been in some form of pain,
It twists and turns the words,
That formulate everything I say.

Every action I take is simply,
an undercurrent of pressure and doubt,
Formed by lies and games,
Carelessly torn from our mouths.

The worst part of it all,
Is that when you take away all these things,
I feel empty and crave the
temptation of relapsing again.

I am not made to be hurt,
and I never wanted to be painted in red,
I'm made for your love,
With my brain craving desire instead.

I've been emptying out my lungs,
Out to a room of soft spoken thoughts,

But they were laden with knives,
And I took all the shots.

If I scream you won't turn,
You've been muted by cruel stab wounds too,
And so I'll run again and again
Until I crash into another fool like you.

MOON, LOVE AND OTHER THINGS...

Taken by a tide, I let you in,
Controlled by the moon, inevitable,
A Fatal Attraction
A misshapen symmetry
Repetitive motions, over and over
The Moon's beauty,
Degraded to a moronic task,
Of making water,
Lap back and forth.
What a waste,
Of a creature,
So above us,
So above love.

Numbed, by still
water, that crushes our veins,

Flooded by rain,
that pours over
your games,

Taken by force,
my forearm,
your bands,

Cut all my hair,
laid out in your
hands,

Do you see, it's not me,

You acquired, in your desire.

To blame it on me would be
disastrous,
My callous heart
Ripped from my chest
Pulling on my right ventricle
That connected, me,
To you.

SEX

When people describe sex as 'fucking'
All emotive responses are degraded
To just,
'Was she tight?' and 'Was he big?'
And people seem to forget that life is literally
formed, by the action they are limiting to just a
'shag'
and purity never came in truer form than when
your eyes lock,
As you are mesmerized by the action of your hips
bumping together,
When the slight hitch of your pleasure escapes in a
moan,
But now it's just a competition,
Of who can 'fuck' the most people, in the most
animalistic of senses.
People disregard the act of two bodies becoming
one,
With the idea of the two bodies coming together,
just to 'cum'
And people take for granted the sensation it can fill
you with,
When grinding turns to frantic fumbling,

And tumbling turns to soft laughter that nothing
else could recreate.

And nothing beats the idea of two brains
connecting,
Flashing across cascades of bright light into each
other's retinas,
A singular, silken tongue that can make a body rise,
Squirm,
Learning where to place your mouth so that their
eyes roll back and their hands turn
the sheets of the bed, into a flowing stream.

But people only see flesh as meat in this generation,
And bodies just become another number,
And it all gets down to who's drunk what, and who's
in luck.

And something that was described as 'making love'
Becomes just who's down to 'fuck'!

SAD MAN

You take on the persona of a sad man,
Quite well.
I see your fickle hands scrunching up,
Paper planes.
Your eyes dart across bodies like, glass marbles.
Do you seek to find another sad,
Reflection like yours?
This sad man mask is cracked and
Flawed.
I see you laugh and snigger even if,
It is at people's pain.
Your body reacts like any others do,
Aching for touch.
You are not a sad man, merely
An uncertain one.
You are not a frenzied shell,
Just merely, a perplex one
This sad man persona must be fucking TIRING.

BUTTERFLY EYED

Butterfly eyed, we did explode,
But the way you lie,
Has a hand round my throat

Chasing cars has never got us far,
And the filtered light, seems,
To want to break my heart

Don't make a sound, or everything,
That we have come across, will
Try to tell us that we are lost

Don't cross those lines,
We both know you're always right

ALIEN

I stroked a bee today,
It lay dormant,
And shy,
I was not hastened to let go.
The birds in the trees,
Seemed distant to me,
I forgot that birds made sound.
I dipped my feet,
Into the icy, moving,
Shallow water,
Realising that I was fucking cold.
It came to my attention,
That I was there,
Alone and surrounded, by
Alien things.
The only things to make me feel alive
For a long time
Who has been touching my skin?
Who have I been letting in?

THE FEAR OF BECOMING OLD

The fear of becoming old consumes me
Seeing sad sunken-in faces plod along,
To the next stop, to the next stop,
Until the next stop is merely death.

I see faithless eyes scour youths,
Wishing 'oh to be young again', and,
Complaining about trivial things,
Such as the stale bread at the supermarket.

I see them holding hands in the streets,
Walking slow in utter silence
As if twenty years of conversation,
Has become a matter of pettiness.

I see lives lived through colourless eyes,
Viewing every regret they have made,
Through the frowns upon their forehead
And the absence of a smile

I do not want to have to wake up
And see that I am shrinking into myself
Becoming an empty sack of bones
Small-talk, and planning Christmas Day

I do not want to have to talk,
On the house telephone with the TV on,

Watching the world slip by and
Accidently calling my daughter by my dog's name.

The fear of becoming old engulfs me
It reminds me of how my time is short
And the days, slow as they are,
Drag you into a religious routine.

Until the next stop, and the next stop
Until I realise that I am dying.

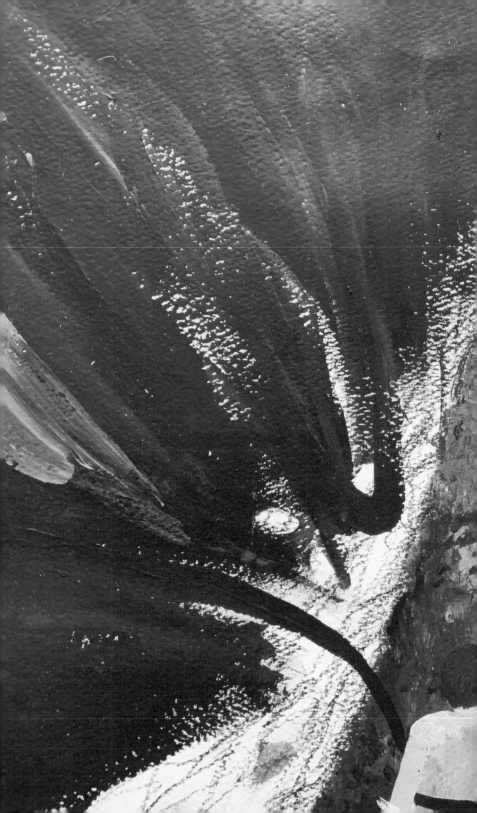

A DIFFERENT LANGUAGE

I sit here in silence
And I look at people's faces
They seem as distant as the moon
What a strange feeling, hearing
Humans in the most animistic of senses,
Senselessly running around with
Futile attempts of keeping their clean exterior, clean

Each person shrouded by their chosen skin
Each person reacting the same but in a different
language
I sit here on the train, in silence,
Everyone speaking their own language
But I must have lost my voice

I sit here on the train,
in silence,
everyone speaking their own language,
I must have lost my voice.

BETH'S 20 RULES OF LIFE

1. You cannot control anyone. Each Human is an individual being. The only thing you can control is how you react to people's actions; thus meaning you can always gain positives from any situation.

2. Get out of Bed! Some days you will feel like crap, and that's ok. Just make sure you at least try to better yourself each and every day; change will come to you.

3. A situation happens that makes you angry, everyone feels angry sometimes. It is about choosing which fights are worth creating energy over. Will it matter tomorrow? In a Week? In a Year? If not, let that shit go.

4. Remain Calm. Too many people let life drag them into a bottomless pit of stress and oppression. Always look at it from an outside perspective; remain chilled and at peace so that this can spread to others.

5. Humans are created imperfect. Each person has positives and negatives, which can also depend on the person that is looking at them. Always look to draw from people how you want to grow, or improve. Always help others grow.

6. Energy. Your energy impacts EVERYONE around you. Always try to outwardly express only pure happiness; as subconsciously people will mirror this feeling, thus making your day 100% better, as you in turn will mirror it back.

7. We cannot always make perfect decisions, as that is how we cope with learning and becoming independent. Do not punish

yourself – learn, grow and teach yourself to say SORRY. (Egos are lame.)

8. Life, in general, is a fascinating thing. Sometimes as a species we forget how blessed we are to be surrounded by beauty and a community. Immerse yourself. Dance, venture out, join a club, Swim in that sea!

9. Love. Love everyone, however hard it is. Love encompasses the whole rotation of life. It may seem cyclical at times, but overall, phenomenal things can be achieved when you love someone, and when they love you back

10. You will only feel good enough when you are at peace with yourself. Confidence is a feeling gained from knowing you have tried your best in a situation. Do not be hard on yourself, do not be too judgmental on others. Do you, and you will reap the benefits

11. Try to remain lighthearted, fun and free. Focusing on materialistic items to the point where it consumes you is unhealthy. Your health, emotions and other people are much more important. Don't lose your sanity or friends.

12. You cannot dictate to people; however easygoing they may be. It is never ok to force your values onto someone else. All you can do is produce a balanced argument and explain your opinion. Let people make their own decisions. You gain respect this way.

13. Do not make rash decisions on temporary emotions. This results in an unbalance of your chakras, and can cause harm to others around you. Focus on your long-term goal, and the rest will fall into place.

14. The more chilled out you are, the easier your ride will be. You need to enjoy yourself, and show others a good time in order to be successful.

15. Do not lose your creativity or 'Spark'. Always find time for what excites you, and makes you an 'individual'. Try to make it a career for yourself.

16. Life is not a competition. Everyone dies, I'm afraid! Help people the fuck out, they could be going against a lot more than you are. A kind gesture is all it takes sometimes. Do not be threatened by the existence of a completely different human being.

17. Smile... at Everyone. You cannot kill someone with kindness.

18. Make sure that everything you create is beautiful; even if all you think it is, is beautifully ugly! Burn that book to let go, but make origami out of it later. Create beautiful sex, create beautiful minds, create beautiful experiences; for yourself but also for others.

19. Always be honest, with yourself and others. In a sea of faces, loneliness springs from distancing yourself from reality and people. Lies will only push you away further. Get a grip, coming to terms with the truth will ultimately lead to a clear head and existence.

20. Be INTENSE.... With everything you care about. Life is too short to float about. You were born to achieve great things. Travel, confess your feelings, act on your emotions, and make plans with people you love. The more you are open with people, the more pleasure you will get back.

IN MEMORY

Beth was unapologetically authentic. She was herself at all times. Her talent and creative flair was sometimes overshadowed by her glamour and cheeky banter. Beth was a wonderful generous person. She always took time with people and made a specific effort to give them what they needed. You could go to Beth with an inkling of an idea, a tiny little notion about something and she would nurture it and grow the idea with you until it was fully fledged.

Beth's wardrobe was HUGE, she was so naturally beautiful but Beth preferred to AMP it up to the Max. I can picture her wrinkled nose snorting laughing while showing off a new tattoo or piercing. She was great for bringing so much colour to our corner of the room. Honestly the boy drama was essential for a Monday tea session!

Beth was more talented than she realised, she was braver then she knew and her potential was huge.

I'm so glad that her manager was Amy, and that Beth started to see the value we all could and knew that we wanted to adopt her into our Google family.

Beth you were 100% adopted, adored and we miss you so much

XXX

Catherine Forrest

CPSIA information can be obtained
at www.ICGtesting.com
Printed in the USA
LVHW070207031120
670490LV00002B/18